D1254766

J 577 .586 TOC
Tocci, Salvatore.
Arctic tundra : life at
the North Pole /

PALM BEACH COUNTY
LIBRARY SYSTEM
3650 SUMMIT BLVD.
WEST PALM BEACH, FLORIDA 33406

Arctic Tundra
Life at the North Pole

Arctic Tundra
Life at the North Pole

Salvatore Tocci

Franklin Watts
A Division of Scholastic Inc.
New York • Toronto • London • Auckland • Sydney
Mexico City • New Delhi • Hong Kong
Danbury, Connecticut

For my daughter Kerri

Note to readers: Definitions for words in **bold** can be found in the Glossary at the back of this book.

Photographs © 2005: Alaska Stock Images: 19 (Jeff Schultz), 49 (Jim Wark); Bryan and Cherry Alexander Photography: 50; Corbis Images: 8 (Bettmann), 41 (Darrell Gulin), 2 (Chris Rainier), 6 (Galen Rowell); Dembinsky Photo Assoc.: 12 (E.R. Degginger), 33 (DPA), 5 left, 16, 17 (Stan Osolinski), 15 (Pekka Parviainen), 52 (Rob Stapleton), 46 (Mark J. Thomas); Peter Arnold Inc.: 44, 53 (Fred Bruemmer), cover, 24, 25, 42, 54 bottom (S.J. Krasemann); Photo Researchers, NY: 54 top (Scott Camazine), 36 (Fletcher & Baylis), 22 (Dan Guravich), 28 (Ted Kerasote), 34 (Steve Krasemann), 5 right, 30, 31, 38, 51 (Tom & Pat Leeson), 29 (Renee Lynn), 21 (Charlie Ott), 23 (Doug Plummer), 26 (Lee F. Snyder).

Illustrations by: XNR Productions, Inc.: 10; Bob Italiano: 14, 45

The photograph on the cover shows the snow-covered tundra. The photograph opposite the title page shows pack ice near the North Pole.

Library of Congress Cataloging-in-Publication Data

Tocci, Salvatore.
    Arctic tundra / Salvatore Tocci.—1st ed.
        p. cm. — (Biomes and habitats)
    Includes bibliographical references (p.).
    ISBN 0-531-12366-9 (lib. bdg.)   0-531-16697-X (pbk.)
    1. Tundra ecology—Arctic regions—Juvenile literature. I. Title. II. Series.
QH541.5.T8T63 2005
577.5'86—dc22

                                        2004013283

©2005 by Salvatore Tocci.
All rights reserved. Published simultaneously in Canada.
Printed in the United States of America.
1 2 3 4 5 6 7 8 9 10 R 14 13 12 11 10 09 08 07 06 05

Contents

The North Pole is encircled by a part of the world called the arctic tundra.

Sitting on Top of the World

On April 6, 1909, Matthew Henson greeted Robert Peary by saying, "I think I'm the first man to sit on top of the world." The two men had finally reached the North Pole after trekking across more than 400 miles (640 kilometers) of ice.

Henson made his claim to fame because he had arrived about forty-five minutes ahead of Peary. Henson could make another claim. He was the first African American to reach the North Pole.

Matthew Henson was orphaned at age eleven and took his first sea voyage at age twelve.

Reaching the North Pole was an incredible challenge. In fact, the two men were forced back in an earlier attempt. They simply could not get past the drifting ice packs. Most people picture this part of the world as being permanently covered

8

with a thick, hard, smooth ice sheet. However, this is not the case. Currents in the water constantly break apart the ice. Some of the ice can be forced upward to form small, steep mountains called pressure ridges. Breaks in the ice also create areas of open water called leads. On his way to the North Pole, Henson once slipped into a lead and had to be rescued.

Henson died on March 9, 1955, at the age of eighty-eight and was buried in New York City. In 1988, his remains were moved to Arlington National Cemetery, just outside Washington, D.C. On his tomb are inscribed the words "The lure of the Arctic is tugging at my heart." Henson had fallen in love with a part of the world known as the **arctic tundra**.

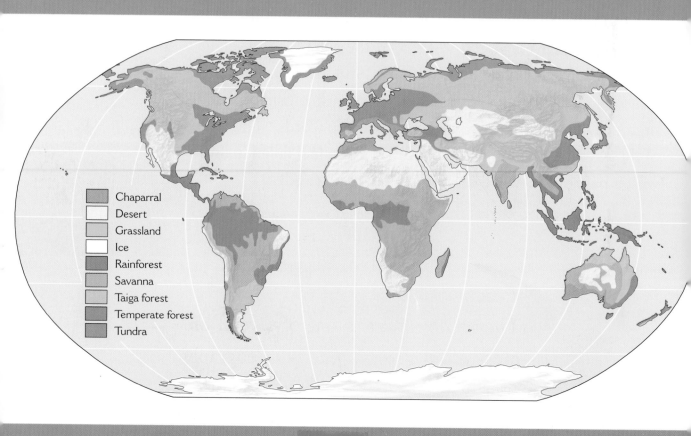

Chaparral
Desert
Grassland
Ice
Rainforest
Savanna
Taiga forest
Temperate forest
Tundra

Antarctica is the only place on Earth without a biome.

Chapter One

The Land of the Midnight Sun

The arctic tundra is one of several **biomes** on Earth. A biome is a geographic area whose environmental conditions determine the kinds of plants and animals that can live in it. These conditions include how much sunlight and precipitation a biome receives.

The name *arctic tundra* provides a clue as to what the environment in this biome is like. *Arctic* indicates that this biome is found in the far northern regions of Earth. *Tundra* may come from a Russian word that means "land of no trees." *Tundra* may also come from a Finnish word that means "barren hill." You can tell from these definitions that the arctic tundra is a treeless, hilly biome.

The Arctic Circle

The arctic tundra forms a huge cap of land around the top of Earth. The center of this cap lies at the North Pole. This cap reaches down to form the Arctic Circle, which runs through northern Canada, Greenland, Norway, Russia, and Alaska. In all, the arctic tundra spreads across some 3 million square miles (about 8 million square km) of land.

Most globes have a line drawn at 66 degrees latitude called the Arctic Circle. North of this line, the sun never sets on June 21 and never rises on December 21. However, the Arctic Circle is actually an imaginary line that changes with time. The

Farther South

A different tundra biome, known as the alpine tundra, exists high in various mountain ranges that are located as far south as Australia.

The arctic tundra makes up about 20 percent of the land on Earth.

exact location of this line of latitude is determined by how Earth spins on its axis as it revolves around the sun.

However, Earth is constantly wobbling as it spins on its axis. This wobble means that Earth tilts slightly toward the sun at certain times and slightly away from the sun at other times. The tilt changes about 2.5 degrees over a period of twenty thousand years. As Earth's tilt changes, so does the location of the Arctic Circle. A 2.5-degree change in Earth's tilt means about a 200-mile (32-km) change in the location of the Arctic Circle every twenty thousand years. The location of the Arctic Circle moves about 25 feet (8 meters) every year.

No Sunsets and No Sunrises

Different places on Earth receive different amounts of sunlight, depending on the season. Days are usually longer in summer and shorter in winter. You read that the sun never sets on June 21 north of the Arctic Circle. Near the North Pole, the sun never sets during all of June and July. During these two months, the days do not end. If the skies are clear, the sun shines even at midnight.

Although the sun may be shining twenty-four hours a day, it never climbs very high in the sky. As a result, sunlight strikes the arctic tundra at an angle rather than directly. This means that, compared to other biomes, the arctic tundra does not receive as much heat from the sun's rays. As a result, summers in the arctic tundra never get very warm.

Winters in the arctic tundra are a different story. You read

The Arctic Circle

Earth is tilted about 24 degrees on its axis. Subtract 24 degrees from 90 degrees, and you get 66 degrees. As a result, the Arctic Circle is drawn on globes and maps as a line around Earth at 66 degrees latitude.

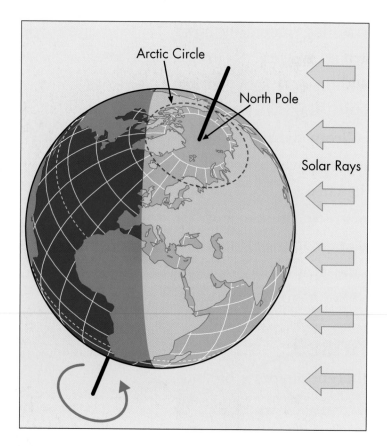

As Earth spins on its axis, it's always daytime in parts of the arctic tundra during most of the summer and always nighttime during most of the winter.

that the sun never rises on December 21 north of the Arctic Circle. Near the North Pole, the sun never rises during all of December and January. Even though the sun does not rise during these two months, it does not get completely dark. Some sunlight reaches this part of the world by bouncing off the atmosphere. The sun rises during the other winter months, but it remains low in the horizon, just as it does in summer.

The arctic tundra has its sunless days in winter and its midnight sun in summer because of Earth's tilt. In winter, Earth is tilted so that the sun's rays cannot reach that part of the world. In summer, Earth is tilted so that this part of the world never moves completely out of the sun's rays.

The Northern Lights

The arctic tundra is a good place to see the northern lights, which are bands of colored lights that streak across the night sky. The closer you get to the North Pole, the more often you will see them on nights that are dark and clear. In northern Norway, they can be seen almost every night. In Alaska, they can be seen between five and ten times a month. Even along the border between the United States and Canada, the northern lights can be seen two to four times a year.

The northern lights are caused by the sun. Explosions and flares are constantly erupting from the surface of the sun. These explosions and flares hurl huge amounts of solar particles into space. These particles are attracted to Earth's magnetic north and south poles. On their way toward the poles, the particles pass through Earth's atmosphere. As they do, they collide with the gases that make up the atmosphere.

Each collision produces a tiny spark of light. Because there are billions of collisions, enough sparks are produced to light up the night sky. In addition to white light, streaks of red and green are also seen as part of the northern lights. All this light is known as an **aurora**. This is why scientists call the northern lights the aurora borealis.

The different colors of the aurora borealis are the result of solar particles colliding with the different gases that make up the atmosphere.

*Winds in the arctic tundra
can result in a wind chill
temperature near
−100 degrees Fahrenheit
(−73 degrees Celsius).*

Chapter Two

A Frozen Land

Henson and Peary were not the first people to try to reach the North Pole. Many explorers had tried before Peary and Henson and failed. Some died while trying. Most of those who survived did not escape unharmed. Their fingers and toes often became frostbitten from exposure to the extreme cold and had to be removed. The arctic tundra is the coldest of all the biomes.

Henson and Peary started their journey to the North Pole on Ellesmere Island, which is located in the tundra of northern Canada. This island, like the rest of the arctic tundra, is covered with

Way Up North

Ellesmere Island is the tenth-largest island in the world and also the northernmost landmass in North America.

snow and ice for most of the year. Most people picture the tundra as a place where it is almost always snowing. In fact, this biome receives little snow or other precipitation, such as sleet or rain.

A Polar Desert

The arctic tundra is sometimes called a polar desert. Both the arctic tundra and a desert are very dry. The arctic tundra gets only 4 to 20 inches (10 to 50 centimeters) of precipitation a year, mostly in the form of snow. This is about the same amount of precipitation that a desert gets in a year in the form of rain. The tundra is covered with snow for seven or eight months a year because the temperature rarely gets warm enough to melt it.

In winter, temperatures range from –70 to 20 degrees F (–57 to –7 degrees C). Winds that often blow from 30 to 60 miles per hour (48 to 96 km per hour) make it feel even colder. These winds can cause "whiteouts" in which the snow blows so much that it is almost impossible to see. Whiteouts sometimes brought Peary and his men to a halt because of the danger of falling into a hole in the ice that they could not see.

In summer, the temperature ranges between 30 degrees and 50 degrees F (–1 and 10 degrees C), which is warm enough to melt the snow. However, the temperature does not get warm enough for much of the water to evaporate. In addition, the water from the melting snow cannot seep very far into the ground because of what lies beneath the surface.

Blowing snow can make it impossible to see in the arctic tundra.

Getting Warmer?

During the 1990s, the U.S. Navy used instruments aboard its nuclear submarines to measure the thickness of the arctic ice. Even in winter, the ice was found to be only a few inches thick in some places and almost 10 feet (3 m) thick in others. The researchers also found that the ice was getting, on average, about 4 inches (10 cm) thinner per year. The arctic ice might be melting because of milder temperatures caused by global warming.

The Permafrost

Any water from rain or melting snow cannot seep into the ground because of the **permafrost**. The permafrost is a thick layer of frozen ground that is the most distinctive feature of the arctic tundra. The permafrost starts between 12 inches (30 cm) and 10 feet (3 m) beneath the surface. From there, it can extend more than 2,000 feet (610 m) into the ground.

The permafrost remains frozen throughout the year and prevents water from seeping deep into the ground. Even in warmer weather, very little of the water that remains above or close to the surface evaporates. Remember that sunlight strikes the tundra's surface at an angle and therefore does not supply much heat to evaporate the water.

Above the permafrost is a thin layer of soil that also freezes during the colder months. This top layer is known as the **active layer** because of the activity that takes place in it during the warmer months, when this soil layer is not frozen. The active layer is used by both animals and plants. Animals

burrow in the active layer to seek shelter and warmth. Plants absorb **nutrients**, such as minerals, that are stored in the active layer. Nutrients are substances that living things need to survive and grow.

Nutrients, however, are found in very limited quantities in the active layer. Dead animals and plants do not decompose very well in the tundra because of the cold weather. As a result, nutrients from their bodies are not returned to the soil. In addition, rocks in the tundra do not weather or erode much because of the cold temperatures. For this reason, these rocks do not contribute many nutrients to the soil.

In summer, water from melting snow causes the arctic land to become soggy in many places.

Pingos and Polygons

Some areas of the arctic tundra are flat. However, rolling hills and broad valleys cover much of the biome. In warmer weather, shallow ponds, deep lakes, narrow rivers, and swampy marshes are found nearly everywhere. In addition, the repeated cycle of freezing and thawing of the active layer creates some interesting land features. One such feature is known as a **pingo**. A pingo is a hill with a hole or crater in its center. When viewed from the air, a pingo looks like a tiny volcano.

Pingos are formed when water in the active layer freezes. Water expands as it freezes. However, the permafrost prevents the freezing water from expanding downward. So the only place for it to expand is upward. The freezing water in the active layer pushes upward on the surface of Earth. Each year, the ground may be pushed upward only a few inches. However, over time, a pingo can grow to be as high as 100 feet (30 m) and as wide as 1,000 feet (305 m).

A bird's-eye view of the tundra also reveals another feature. In flat areas, the land seems to be carved into irregular shapes. When viewed from the air, each shape is a many-sided figure

No Trees

The shallowness and lack of nutrients in the active layer are two reasons why trees cannot grow in the arctic tundra.

Pingos form mainly in the tundra where lakes and rivers are found.

Each polygon is so large that it is not noticeable from the ground.

that can be from 10 to 100 feet (3 to 30 m) wide. These land features are called **polygons** because they consist of figures with many sides. Like pingos, polygons are formed by the repeated freezing and thawing of the active layer.

The ice and cold shape not only the tundra landscape but also the kinds of animals and plants that can live there. For example, the ice and cold prevent many kinds of animals from living in the tundra. Instead, these animals just visit when the weather gets warmer.

An adult tundra swan can weigh more than 20 pounds (9 kilograms) and have a wingspan of 7 feet (2 m).

Chapter Three

The Visitors

The scientists were hiding in the bushes in a field in Pennsylvania. Suddenly, they fired small rockets that were attached to a large net. As the rockets soared through the air, they spread the large net over the field. When the rockets landed, the net fell down to the ground. Trapped under the net were large, white birds called tundra swans.

The scientists carefully removed the swans from the net and placed plastic collars around some of the birds' necks. A small radio transmitter was attached to each collar that would allow the scientists to track a swan. Each spring, these swans

Frequent Flier Miles

The average life span of an arctic tern is twenty years. During this time, a tern will have flown roughly 440,000 miles (704,000 km).

An arctic tern weighs less than 1 pound (454 grams) and is only about 12 to 15 inches (30 to 38 cm) long.

fly almost 4,000 miles (6,400 km). They spend the winter in U.S. coastal areas along both the Atlantic and Pacific Oceans. When spring arrives, millions of swans fly to the arctic tundra in northern Alaska and northwestern Canada, where they breed.

Flying In

In addition to arctic swans, other birds also fly to the tundra in summer. These include geese, ducks, gulls, loons, and sandpipers. The record, however, for the bird that makes the longest trip to visit the tundra belongs to the arctic tern. These birds fly more than 22,000 miles (32,000 km) from the Antarctic near the South Pole to the arctic tundra and back each year. This is the longest annual trip made by any living thing on Earth.

Terns usually arrive in the tundra in May. They soon choose mates and begin nesting. Their nests are little more than shallow depressions dug into the ground near water. A

female usually lays two eggs that hatch in about twenty-three days. The young leave their nest soon after hatching and hide in the grass for protection. Their parents provide them with small fish to eat. In about twenty-five days, the young are ready to fly. Less than three months after their arrival, the terns begin their long journey back to Antarctica.

Walking In

In April, large animals known as caribou begin their migration to the arctic tundra. They spend winters in a biome known as the **taiga**. Located south of the tundra, a taiga contains evergreen forests of pine and fir trees. As warmer weather approaches, the caribou may travel hundreds of miles to the tundra.

After they arrive in the tundra, the caribou live in small groups. Females give birth in early June. During the several

The Great Migration

During the eighteenth and nineteenth centuries, explorers reported seeing millions of caribou migrating across the arctic tundra. As they migrated, the caribou were hunted and killed. As a result, their population decreased dramatically. However, caribou still make up one of the largest herds of animals that migrate, numbering in the hundreds of thousands.

Reaching the tundra involves crossing rivers. Caribou hair is hollow and filled with air. Their hair acts like a life jacket, allowing the caribou to float as they swim across the water. Caribou are excellent swimmers. They can also walk on deep snow. Caribou have four hoofed "toes" on each foot that they spread apart to act like snowshoes.

These animals are called caribou in the North American tundra and reindeer in the Scandinavian and Siberian tundra.

weeks they spend in the tundra, the caribou eat as much as possible to prepare for the winter. They feed on tundra plants, including flowers and leaves. A bull, or male caribou, can gain as much as 60 pounds (27 kg) in this time and weigh between 275 and 600 pounds (125 and 270 kg). A cow, or female caribou, weighs between 200 and 300 pounds (90 and 135 kg).

Following Along

Along their migration route through the arctic tundra, the caribou do not travel alone. Tundra wolves follow along. These wolves live in packs of five to fifteen animals. Each pack has a leader, which can be either a male or a female wolf. A wolf's favorite meal is caribou meat.

Unlike the caribou, wolves live year-round in the tundra. As the caribou pass through on their migration, the wolves chase and kill them. Most caribou are fast and can escape. In addition, the caribou can defend themselves with their antlers and hooves. For these reasons, the wolves seek out the younger, older, weaker, or slower caribou. Still, only about one in ten chases results in a wolf capturing a caribou. Because the caribou are so big, weeks may pass before a successful hunter wolf needs to go after another one.

Wolves are not the only problem the caribou encounter during their migration. Swarms of mosquitoes travel with the herd. Female mosquitoes are the main problem. A swarm of female mosquitoes can take as much as 1 quart (1.1 liter) of blood from a single caribou in a week. During their migration, the caribou make side trips to coastal areas, where strong winds blow away many of the mosquitoes. However, each trip may add as many as 50 miles (80 km) a day to a caribou's journey.

Losing blood and traveling extra miles during their migration weaken many of the caribou. This makes them easier targets for the wolves. The wolves' hunting keeps the caribou population from getting too big. You read that a caribou has a tremendous appetite for plants. If the caribou population were to get too large, there would be far fewer plants growing in the tundra.

Their white fur makes tundra wolves difficult to spot in the snow-covered tundra.

Tundra plants are colorful and grow low to the ground, where it is warmer.

Chapter Four

Tundra Plants

With a soil that is poor in nutrients and temperatures that are rarely warm, the arctic tundra does not seem like a place where many plants can grow. Yet certain plants do thrive in the tundra. Like those in any other biome, plants in the tundra must have the **adaptations** needed to survive. An adaptation is a feature that increases a living thing's chances of survival. Tundra plants share similar adaptations.

Tundra plants have shallow roots that spread through the active layer of the soil. Tundra plants are also short and have as much of their mass belowground, in their root systems, as they do aboveground. Growing tall in the tundra is almost a sure way for a plant to die from exposure to the cold. This is why tundra plants are so short.

Tundra plants are almost all **perennials**. A perennial plant is one that lives for more than two growing seasons. Most perennials keep their leaves over the winter. Those that lose their leaves store nutrients in their stems and roots before winter arrives. As a result, perennials can start developing new growth as soon as the weather gets warmer. In contrast, a plant that starts from seed would never be able to grow to maturity during the short growing season.

Lichens and Mosses

Growing on the tundra are living things called lichens, which look like plants, but are actually not. A **lichen** is made up of two **organisms**, or living things. One is an alga and the other is a fungus. Neither the alga nor the fungus is a plant because neither has roots, stems, or leaves. The alga, however, is similar to a plant in that it makes food through a process called **photosynthesis**. Photosynthesis is the process by which plants use sunlight, water, and carbon dioxide to make oxygen and food, such as sugars. This food is also used by the fungus, which provides shelter and protection for the alga.

Lichens are among the hardiest tundra organisms, growing on rocks and bare soil. Although lichens grow very slowly,

A Short Season

The growing season for tundra plants lasts only ten to fourteen weeks each year.

A Misleading Name

Caribou moss, which caribou eat in large quantities, is actually a lichen, not a moss.

they can live for hundreds of years. Their long life span enables them to form huge, colorful splotches that cover the tundra landscape.

A variety of mosses, which are a type of plant, grow in the tundra. Mosses are simple plants that grow as thick, green, tightly packed mats that are close to the ground. These mats can be so thick that walking on them feels like walking on a soft mattress. An example is sphagnum moss. This moss comes in various colors, with pale green being the most common. Sphagnum moss can absorb water from the moisture in the air. Its ability to retain moisture is the reason why people sometimes grow sphagnum moss together with water-loving plants, such as orchids.

In addition to pale green, sphagnum moss comes in shades of yellow, pink, red, and brown.

Sedges and Grasses

Perennials that grow in the tundra include sedges and grasses. Sedges look like grasses except that they have hollow, rather than solid, stems. Neither type of plant grows very tall. A sedge commonly found in the tundra is the arctic cotton. The stem of this plant grows to be about 1 foot (30 cm) high and is topped with a white, silky fluff. Long ago, people living on the tundra collected these soft fluffs to line their boots and stuff their mattresses.

Although they are much smaller, tussocks are formed in the same way pingos are.

Another tundra sedge is called *Kobresia*, which grows quickly but gets no taller than a person's hand. Like all sedges, *Kobresia* can absorb water from the ground much faster than other plants can. It also has the ability to absorb certain nutrients that other plants cannot. This is an important adaptation that allows it to survive in the nutrient-poor soil of the tundra. Being so well adapted to the tundra environment has enabled some *Kobresia* plants to live for more than two hundred years.

Although they are short, grasses can make walking through parts of the tundra a challenge. In marshy areas, the repeated freezing and thawing of water create small mounds known as **tussocks**. These mounds, which look like rounded hills, are made entirely of plants. One plant that makes up these tussocks is appropriately called tussock grass. Tussocks break the wind and expose more plants to the sun. This helps warm the grasses.

Flowers and Shrubs

Summer is the time when flowering perennials splatter the tundra with a variety of colors. These flowering plants include yellow poppies, lavender louseworts, pink fireweeds, and pale cream mountain avens. Each plant is adapted to meet the challenge of reaching its full growth in a rather short time. For example, the flowers of the mountain avens always point toward the sun, which helps them grow as quickly as possible. In addition, the flower parts form a cup-shaped dish that acts as a solar energy collector. This natural solar panel concentrates the sun's rays onto the center of the flower. Insects often

Tea Leaves

Another flowering plant is the Labrador tea, which is an unusual arctic plant because it can grow as tall as 5 feet (1.5 m). The leaves and sometimes the twigs and flowers are used to make tea. The tea made from this arctic plant has a high vitamin C content. Many people take vitamin C to prevent colds. The leaves of Labrador tea are also scattered among clothes to chase away moths.

People living in the North American tundra call the mountain avens "the follower" because it always points toward the sun.

warm themselves inside these flowers before heading out into the cooler arctic air.

A common shrub that grows in the tundra is the arctic willow. This shrub grows in clumps that form dense mats. These willows can spread out to cover broad areas with their fairly large leaves and sparkling pink flowers that blossom in summer. In addition to flowers, some shrubs that grow on the tundra produce berries that can be eaten. These include cranberries, blueberries, bearberries, and crowberries. Bearberries are commonly eaten by bears, and crowberries are commonly eaten by crows. Berries are just one source of food that plants provide for the tundra animals. In fact, without arctic plants, there would be no tundra animals.

*A musk ox can grow
to be 900 pounds
(410 kg) by eating
only tiny tundra plants.*

Chapter Five

Tundra Animals

Like all biomes, the tundra is a living community of organisms. Plants are the **producers** because they use the energy from sunlight to make food. A producer is an organism that can make its own food. Animals are the **consumers** because they cannot make their own food. A consumer is an organism that depends on another organism for food. It eats either plants or animals, or both. Food provides the energy that all organisms need to live and reproduce.

Predators

In a food chain, animals other than the primary consumers are also called predators.

Energy always flows from the sun to producers and then to consumers. The organisms in this flow of energy make up a **food chain**. A food chain describes the feeding relationships of organisms. In a food chain, one organism is eaten by another organism, which is then eaten by another organism, and so on. Animals that feed upon plants are known as **primary consumers**. Those that feed upon primary consumers are called **secondary consumers**. A food chain continues when those next in line feed upon the secondary consumers, and so on.

Primary Consumers

One of the most interesting adaptations to the arctic cold can be seen in a primary consumer known as the woolly bear. Despite its name, this animal is not a bear. The woolly bear is a caterpillar that grows to be about the size of your thumb. During the winter, the woolly bear produces chemicals that act like antifreeze to prevent ice from forming inside its body. The woolly bear remains inactive during the winter. In spring, the woolly bear starts to stir. For one month in summer, this tiny insect grows a little bit by getting nutrients from the leaves it eats. In fall, the woolly bear again prepares for winter. This cycle continues for about fourteen years until the caterpillar is finally large enough to change into a moth. The moth breeds and then dies within a few weeks.

Woolly bears are just one type of insect that lives in the tundra. In fact, insects are among the most numerous inhabitants of the tundra. These insects include flies, moths, butterflies, and bees. Most of these tiny animals are primary consumers that feed on the sugary nectar of tundra plants.

Larger primary consumers include squirrels, mice, voles, hares, and lemmings. These animals are also found in warmer biomes. However, those living in the arctic tundra look quite different. For example, their legs, ears, and tails are shorter than those of similar animals that live in warmer climates. This adaptation reduces the chances that these body parts will get frostbitten. Shorter body parts also lose less heat to the surrounding air.

These animals are adapted to the tundra in other ways. Ground squirrels, for example, eat as much as possible during the summer and store the excess as fat. When winter arrives, they

The chemicals inside a woolly bear's body protect it against temperatures as cold as –95 degrees F (–70 degrees C).

The ground squirrel is the only tundra animal that truly hibernates in winter.

hibernate in underground burrows. Hibernation involves slowing down all body functions so that they almost come to a stop. During hibernation, a ground squirrel's heart rate will slow down from two hundred beats per minute to ten beats per minute.

The largest primary consumers found in the tundra include caribou, bighorn sheep, Siberian ibex, and musk oxen. The tundra is the only biome in which musk oxen are found. In fact, they live there year-round. Their thick fur and large amount of body fat enable them to live in the tundra in the winter.

Secondary Consumers

An example of a secondary consumer is the arctic fox, which feeds mainly on lemmings. An arctic fox has two layers of thick fur. The inner layer is very soft and insulates the fox against the cold. The outer layer is made from hairs that shed water and keep the fox dry. In summer, the fox's fur is brown. In winter, it is white. This change of color allows the fox to blend in with its surroundings and increases its chances of success when it hunts for food. The fox uses its sense of smell to detect a lemming, even one hiding under the snow. Using its strong legs, the fox breaks through the snow to trap the lemming.

Lemmings are also eaten by other secondary consumers, such as weasels and snowy owls. An adult snowy owl will eat three to five lemmings a day. During the spring mating season, a male owl may kill dozens of lemmings that he piles up in front of a female he is courting. Fortunately, the lemmings can replenish their population despite the huge appetites of their predators. Lemmings are the only tundra animals that reproduce year-round. One female can have hundreds of offspring in just one year.

A secondary consumer, such as a snowy owl, obtains only about 10 percent of the energy available in a primary consumer, such as a lemming. In turn, a lemming obtains only

A Doomed Migration

Lemmings are known for their mass migration, during which many drown while trying to swim across rivers and streams in their search for food.

To maintain its body temperature in winter, a lemming eats up to twice its weight in food every day.

about 10 percent of the energy available in producers. Because so little energy is transferred, each link in a food chain must have many more organisms than the next higher link in the chain. For example, the arctic tundra must have many more lemmings than snowy owls. Scientists refer to these feeding relationships as a **food pyramid** because the number of organisms decreases as you move up through a food chain.

Food Webs

Feeding relationships are not as simple as a food chain might suggest. For example, an animal may be a primary consumer at some times and a secondary consumer at others. A grizzly bear that lives in the tundra functions as a primary consumer when it eats berries. However, the bear becomes a secondary consumer when it feeds upon salmon or caribou, which it does when berries are scarce.

Food chains can not only change but can also be linked to one another to show more complex feeding relationships. These diagrams are known as **food webs**. For example, lemmings, musk oxen, and caribou all eat lichens and grasses.

Both arctic foxes and snowy owls eat lemmings. Grizzly bears feed upon both musk oxen and caribou. The feeding relationships between all these organisms can be diagrammed in a food web.

Another food web involves an animal that is probably the most recognized of all tundra organisms, the polar bear. Polar bears spend most of the year floating on thick ice sheets while they hunt for seals. When the ice sheets get too thin to float on in warmer weather, the bears move

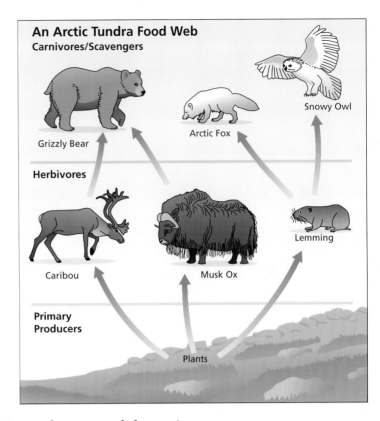

An Arctic Tundra Food Web
Carnivores/Scavengers

Grizzly Bear
Arctic Fox
Snowy Owl

Herbivores

Caribou
Musk Ox
Lemming

Primary Producers

Plants

to the land. There they eat berries, plants, and lemmings. Recently, scientists have discovered that polar bears have become thinner and have given birth to fewer offspring. Scientists have also discovered what is threatening the polar bears and other organisms in the tundra biome.

Changes in the tundra caused by humans may be affecting the welfare of the polar bears.

Chapter Six

A Threatened Biome

Polar bears in the Scandinavian tundra have higher doses of certain toxic chemicals in their bodies than does nearly any other wild animal that has been tested. These toxic chemicals include polychlorinated biphenyl compounds, known simply as PCBs. These chemicals were once used in insulating and cooling fluids in appliances, such as air conditioners and refrigerators. However, scientists discovered that PCBs can damage an animal's nervous system, reduce its chances

Extinction

The woolly mammoth is an animal that once roamed the arctic tundra and other biomes, but is now extinct. Scientists are not sure why this animal became extinct when it did, about ten thousand years ago. Some think humans may have hunted it out of existence. Others think that a change in the climate or the vegetation may have been responsible for its extinction.

of fighting infections, and cause diseases, including cancer. As a result, the use of PCBs was banned in most of the world in the 1970s. By this time, however, PCBs had already escaped into the atmosphere.

Although PCBs were released in many places throughout the world, they were carried by the wind mainly to the atmosphere over the arctic. There the PCBs landed on the snow and ice. They then moved through the arctic food chain, starting with primary consumers and ending with the polar bears.

PCBs are very stable and do not break down. Therefore, PCBs become ten to twenty times more concentrated in each link higher in a food chain. As a result, a polar bear may have a PCB concentration that is a million times greater than the concentration found in the arctic snow.

Scientists are not sure of all the effects that PCBs will have on arctic life, especially the polar bears. Some scientists are concerned that PCBs might lead to the extinction of the polar bear from the Scandinavian tundra. The PCB problem is just one example of how the arctic tundra is threatened as a result of human activities.

The People of the Tundra

During the ice ages, ocean levels rose and fell several times as the climate changed from warm to cold weather. During extended periods of warm weather, ice sheets that covered much of Earth melted. Ocean levels rose as the water from the melting ice poured into the seas. During extended periods of

cold weather, the ice sheets reformed. Ocean levels then dropped as the water froze, and huge amounts of ice and snow were deposited on land.

When the ice sheets reformed, the ocean levels dropped enough to expose land areas that were once covered with water. A land area that was once exposed by low ocean levels was called Beringia. It linked Asia and North America near the present-day Bering Strait located between Siberia and Alaska. This link was a stretch of land perhaps as wide as 1,000 miles (1,600 km). Scientific evidence suggests that this "land bridge" was cool, wet, and grassy. Humans used Beringia to cross from Siberia into Alaska on several different occasions over the past forty thousand years.

The last people to cross Beringia were the Inuit, who entered Alaska between twelve thousand and fifteen thousand

Both the Bering Strait and Beringia are named after Vitus Bering, an eighteenth-century Danish explorer.

Homes in the tundra must be built on stilts. If they touched the ground, the heat from the homes would melt the permafrost. The homes would then sink into the ground.

years ago. The Inuit made their homes near the Arctic Ocean, where they could catch fish to eat. Unlike most other settlers in a new land, the Inuit could not farm the land to raise crops for food. They had to depend on fishing and hunting, along with what berries and edible plants they could collect.

Today, the Inuit are just one of several groups of people who live in the tundra. Others include the Sami in Scandinavia, the Nenets in Siberia, and the Gwich'in in northern Canada. Like all tundra organisms, these people must adapt to the harsh living conditions of the region.

A Hidden Resource

Those who first came to the tundra believed that this land was sacred. Many of those who followed saw the tundra as a land of opportunity. Recently, people have journeyed to the tundra in search of a valuable resource that lies underground. This resource is oil. In the late 1960s, the largest oil field in North America was discovered in the Alaskan tundra. Tall oil rigs now dot the landscape near Prudhoe Bay. A huge pipeline was built to transport the oil nearly 800 miles (1,280 km) from Prudhoe Bay to Prince William Sound, where it is loaded onto oil tankers.

Some sections of the pipeline are below-ground. The above-ground sections were built high enough that caribou can pass underneath them during their migrations.

A balance must be maintained so that this fragile biome is preserved. On one side are the benefits the oil industry brings to the local residents. Many people received large amounts of money from oil companies in exchange for the right to drill on their land. Since oil was first discovered, thousands of jobs have also been created for local residents. This money has enabled the people to build homes and schools, establish health and community services, and purchase modern conveniences.

On the other side are the threats of pollution to the tundra environment. For example, in 1989, an oil tanker named the *Exxon Valdez* ran aground. Millions of gallons of oil spilled into the water, where it clogged the gills of fish. Much of it floated toward shore, where it coated the feathers of birds and

the fur of land animals. The oil killed tens of thousands of animals.

Keeping the benefits and drawbacks provided by drilling for oil in the tundra in balance has recently become an even greater challenge. Oil companies are seeking to drill in Alaska's Arctic National Wildlife Refuge. They believe that this area may be the site of a huge oil deposit. They argue that this oil would bring even greater benefits to the local economy. However, many scientists feel that the threat to the fragile biome this drilling would cause outweighs whatever benefits the oil might provide. Those opposed to drilling believe that this area of the arctic tundra is already seriously threatened.

The oil spill from the Exxon Valdez *affected some 1,000 miles (1,600 km) of coastline, including four wildlife refuges and three national parks.*

Other Threats

When the first humans settled in the tundra, they hunted with spears and arrows they made by hand. In contrast, modern-day hunters started using rifles. The impact on tundra animals was devastating. For example, between three and four million caribou lived in the North American tundra in 1900. By 1950, only two to three hundred thousand were left. To eliminate the threat to the caribou population, laws were passed to limit hunting. Today, the caribou population numbers more than one million.

Other threats to the tundra biome are also being addressed. Although the tundra is not heavily populated, pollution is still a threat. PCBs are just one example. Litter and solid wastes are a problem, just as they are in every other biome. The tundra air is also becoming polluted with substances, such as PCBs, that come from elsewhere. In 1986, radioactive particles from the explosion of a nuclear reactor in the Soviet Union were carried by the wind to the Scandinavian tundra. These particles fell to the ground, where they were taken in by plants. Reindeer that ate these plants then became contaminated.

Global warming is another threat to the arctic tundra. This threat involves an increase in Earth's average temperature. What seems like a small temperature increase can actually have drastic affects. In the arctic tundra, an increase in average temperature would melt the snow cover and the permafrost. Coastal areas all over Earth might flood as a result of this melting. As the climate warms, trees might start growing in the southern parts of the tundra, causing ponds and marshes to be sucked dry by thirsty trees.

A Huge Area

The Arctic National Wildlife Refuge covers about 20 million acres (8 million hectares), an area about the size of South Carolina.

Like his ancestors did, this Inuit boy is using a spear to catch a fish called arctic char.

53

Reindeer are a major source of food for the Sami people who live in the Scandinavian tundra.

The arctic tundra, as it now appears, was formed only about ten thousand years ago, when the last ice age ended.

If global warming continues, the tundra may look like it did some ten thousand years ago, when the last ice age ended. Back then, the plants and animals were different from those that live in the tundra now. Many people are trying to eliminate the threats to the arctic tundra so that this biome remains the living community it is today.

Glossary

active layer—layer of soil in the tundra in which animals burrow and plants establish roots

adaptation—feature that increases an organism's chances of survival

arctic tundra—biome that is centered around the North Pole in which the soil beneath the top layer is permanently frozen

aurora—nighttime lights in the sky caused by particles from the sun passing through Earth's atmosphere

biome—geographic area with certain environmental conditions where certain kinds of plants and animals live

consumer—organism that must consume, or eat, another organism to obtain its food

food chain—diagram that shows the sequence of organisms through which energy flows from producers to consumers

food pyramid—diagram that shows the relative number of organisms in each link of a food chain

food web—diagram that shows several food chains that are associated with one another

lichen—plantlike organism that grows on bare rocks and barren ground

nutrient—substance an organism needs to survive and grow

organism—living thing

perennial—plant that lives for at least two growing seasons

permafrost—layer of permanently frozen ground

photosynthesis—process through which plants make food

pingo—large hill formed by the freezing and thawing of the active layer of soil

polygon—large land area that has the shape of a figure with many sides

primary consumer—organism that eats plants

producer—organism that makes its own food, usually through photosynthesis

secondary consumer—animal that feeds on a primary consumer or another animal that eats plants

taiga—biome south of the arctic tundra in which forests of evergreen trees are common

tussock—small mound that is formed by the freezing and thawing of the active layer of soil and is covered with plants, especially grasses

To Find Out More

Books

Kaplan, Elizabeth. *The Tundra*. Benchmark Books, 1995.

Mudd-Ruth, Maria. *The Tundra*. Benchmark Books, 2000.

Sayre, April Pulley. *Tundra*. 21st Century Books, 1997.

Shepherd, Donna Walsh. *Tundra*. Franklin Watts, 1996.

Organizations and Online Sites

The Arctic
http://www.athropolis.com/links/arctic.htm
This site has numerous links with additional information. You
can learn more about how to make blubber mitts to find out

how animals insulate themselves against the cold and about how to make arctic sun goggles.

Earth Observatory: Tundra
http://earthobservatory.nasa.gov/Laboratory/Biome/biotundra.html
Here you can examine graphs that show changes in temperature and precipitation over the course of one year.

A Food Web in the Tundra
http://curriculum.calstatela.edu/courses/builders/lessons/less/biomes/tundra/tundraweb.html
Read about a tundra food web. Learn what is meant by the term "carrying capacity" and how this affects the numbers of organisms in each food chain.

The Tundra Biome
http://oncampus.richmond.edu/academics/education/projects/webunits/biomes/tundra.html
Links are provided to allow you to read more about the climate, plants, animals, and interesting facts about the tundra.

The Tundra
http://www.brainpop.com/science/ecology/tundra/index.weml
Watch a short movie about the tundra and then take a quiz to test your knowledge about this fragile biome.

A Note on Sources

My interest in the arctic tundra started at an early age, when I became fascinated with the adventures of explorers trying to reach the North Pole. Reading various books about the race between Robert Peary and Frederick Cook to be the first to reach the North Pole revealed how harsh tundra conditions could be.

In carrying out my research for this book, I relied mainly on the Internet to get current information. Only sources that can be considered reliable were used. These included those sponsored by government agencies, wildlife organizations, and educational institutions. Among my travel plans are a visit to the Alaskan tundra, a journey I will make during the summer so that I can see the sun at midnight.

—*Salvatore Tocci*

Index

Numbers in *italics* indicate illustrations.

About the Author

Salvatore Tocci taught high school and college science for almost thirty years. He has a bachelor's degree from Cornell University and a Master of Philosophy degree from The City University of New York. Tocci lives in East Hampton, New York, with his wife Patti.

He has written books that deal with a range of science topics, from biographies about famous scientists to a high school chemistry textbook. He has also traveled throughout the United States to present workshops at national science conventions to show teachers how to emphasize the applications of scientific knowledge to students in their everyday lives.